Hamlet in Exile

Hamlet in Exile

Ulf Kirchdorfer

LITERARY PRESS
LAMAR UNIVERSITY

ISBN: 978-1-942956-83-9
Library of Congress Control Number: 2020944794
Manufactured in the United States

Hamlet on the front cover
taken from a painting by
Harold Copping, 1897

Lamar University Literary Press
Beaumont, Texas

for
Kristin

Recent Poetry from Lamar University Literary Press

Lisa Adams, *Xuai*
Bobby Aldridge, *An Affair of the Stilled Heart*
Michael Baldwin, *Lone Star Heart, Poems of a Life in Texas*
Charles Behlen, *Failing Heaven*
David Bowles, *Flower, Song, Dance: Aztec and Mayan Poetry*
Jerry Bradley, *Collapsing into Possibility*
Jerry Bradley, *Crownfeathers and Effigies*
Jerry Bradley and Ulf Kirchdorfer, editors, *The Great American Wise Ass
    Poetry Anthology*
Matthew Brennan, *One Life*
Mark Busby, *Through Our Times*
Julie Chappell, *Mad Habits of a Life*
Stan Crawford, Resisting Gravity
Chip Dameron, *Waiting for an Etcher*
Glover Davis, *My Mad Cap of Darkness*
William Virgil Davis, *The Bones Poems*
Jeffrey DeLotto, *Voices Writ in Sand*
Chris Ellery, *Elder Tree*
Dede Fox, *On Wings of Silence*
Alan Gann, *That's Entertainment*
Larry Griffin, *Cedar Plums*
Katherine Hoerth, *Goddess Wears Cowboy Boots*
Michael Jennings, *Crossings, a Record of Travel*
Betsy Joseph, *Only So Many Autumns*
Lynn Hoggard, *Motherland*
Gretchen Johnson, *A Trip Through Downer, Minnesota*
Ulf Kirchdorfer, *Chewing Green Leaves*
Laozi, *Daodejing*, tr. By David Breeden, Steven Schroeder, and Wally Swist
Janet McCann, *The Crone at the Casino*
Erin Murphy, *Ancilla*
Laurence Musgrove, *Local Bird*
Benjamin Myers, *Black Sunday*
Godspower Oboido, *Wandering Feet on Pebbled Shores*
Dave Oliphant, *The Pilgrimage, Selected Poems: 1962-2012*
Kornelijus Platelis, *Solitary Architectures*
Carol Coffee Reposa, *Underground Musicians*
Jan Seale, *The Parkinson Poems*
Steven Schroeder, *the moon, not the finger, pointing*
Glen Sorestad *Hazards of Eden*
Vincent Spina, *The Sumptuous Hills of Gulfport*
W.K. Stratton, *Ranchero Ford/ Dying in Red Dirt Country*
Gary Swaim, *Quixotic Notions*
Wally Swist, *Invocation*
Waldman, Ken, *Sports Page*
Loretta Diane Walker, *Ode to My Mother's Voice*
Dan Williams, *Past Purgatory, a Distant Paradise*
Jonas Zdanys, *The Angled Road*
Jonas Zdanys (ed.), *Pushing the Envelope, Epistolary Poems*
Jonas Zdanys, *Red Stones*
Jonas Zdanys, *Three White Horses*

For information on these and other Lamar University Literary Press books go to
www.Lamar.edu/literarypress

Acknowledgments

I much appreciate Jerry Bradley for allowing me onto his lawn to rest a spell in the shade. There he graciously made time to read and "get" what I was doing instead of getting a shotgun out and telling me to get off his lawn. Thanks to the poet Sherry Craven, my letter-companion in bird enthusiasm, "Hamleteering,"for her frequent encouragement that somehow made its way transformed into some of the poems. Howard Stiller, thank you for keeping the hounds at bay as much as possible while I worked on this project.

Thank you Laurence Musgrove for starting the webzine TEJAS-COVIDO and allowing Hamlet to appear on Jeopardy in his electronic pages when I looked up to take a break from this all-consuming project.

I appreciate the editors and book designers of Lamar University Literary Press for their encouragement and support, along with occasional tugging on the reins when I and the project really needed it. The editors had faith in me all along as I came up with the idea of writing a book of poems featuring Hamlet that would engage with Shakespeare's play closely and also move further afield. It is not every day that an author can pitch a project of writing Hamlet poems and be met by enthusiasm, especially during times of fiscal captivity and other pressures on publishers. At no time did I feel the pressure to write "well-behaved," surefire poems for literary journals.

I am grateful for the friendship of Frank Kersnowski, whom I first met when I took his poetry writing class at Trinity University a very long time ago. Frank is the one I lovingly blame for my entering the world of poetry and never leaving.

Bob Flynn (*Robert* Flynn on his many book covers) since the very early 1980s has been a good friend, patiently reading my writing, which is very different from his. In a saintly way (I am sure he will object theologically and philosophically, as well as humorously, to the use of this term), he allowed me in his writing seminar to go full blast and write a postmodern novel set in the jungles of Conrad's *Heart of Darkness* with a Hamlet character and a young man's intense interest in the Oedipus complex. For two semesters I rebelliously took on modernism, just having discovered postmodernism and worshiping it.

John Brantley, a wonderful professor, human being, and aficionado of postmodern fiction, somehow had me reading *Gravity's Rainbow* while I was in Mexico on spring break. Such was John's influence, extending to my neglect of most temptations offered there: blame it all on John and Pynchon.

I am grateful to my students over the years who so often gave me more than they will ever know.

My only brother knows why I thank him.

Kristin I will never be able to thank enough.

CONTENTS

Hamlet Fishing

Cast out the line and be content
where it lands. Let the bobber float,
dance up and down if it is in your mind,
tug a little if you absolutely must.
Ascertain if fish are nibbling
or your thoughts turn to phantoms even
when you should empty your mind.
For God's sake, do you need someone
not to spare the rod, does Calvin (not
the Hobbes kind) need to accompany you
fishing? Does every bird on the wing have to be
prey or falcon? Can you just this once clear your
mind and cast and bring in the line so something
solid like peace or a fish touches your antic self?

Sea-Gown Ahoy!

The eloquence of words, as if Hamlet
had really spoken them, "My sea-gown
scarfed about me," as I walk through
the rain shielded by foldable umbrella
too small to protect legs stepping ahead.
Had Hamlet deployed an umbrella that night
he threw caution to hell and finally struck
with the pen to avoid having his dibbing head
chopped off, might even have ordered a burger
with cheese and bacon if his puppeteer's anachronisms
had allowed it, but no, he had to go back
to the royal wine bar for twits, with Claudius
concocting a drinking game to end the play,
obedient Hamlet stuck and struck full stop ahead.

Only Connect

Hamlet at dusk—
or is it dawn—
at the ESSO station
running into Hopper
posing as a gas attendant.
"Not everything can be perfect,"
he volunteers while filling
up Hamlet's car. Hamlet lights
a cig and offers Hopper a smoke.
"We have to live dangerously,"
pumping Edward grins and lets
Hamlet give him a light.
It turns out it was Hemingway,
not Hopper. Misremembrance is a gift.

Kite-Flying

The throbbing of ink in my ears.
Pulse in the pillow, rain and thunder
outside the castle. I wake up thinking
Rosencrantz and Guildenstern are flying kites
in this mess, lightning their string, what will
happen to my playmates. Who are their
parents? Conversations stopping like hens' heads
severed when I enter the room. Did they
not have the same wet-nurse as I? I look for
features in them, when I squint or frame a moment
of their faces, I think my father, my mother,
uncle, the weather is bad, should I go outside
and rescue my friends unspooling kites as if they
were fish at the other end of the line?

Bearish

You cannot expect Hamlet
to be the same Hamlet
wherever he travels. Today
he is an explorer wearing protective
eye gear meant for Arctic explorers.
The whole outfit, the way most of us
imagine it. He has not stepped out
to greet Penguins or a Polar Bear.
But it is only a matter of time
before he walks in awkward posture
toward the frozen bear float without
bars, the off-white bear angry
the ice has split and hunting is bad.
Hamlet is on the tip of the tongue of the bear.

The Boy Who Would Not Play Rough

Hamlet, are you bird-scoping again? I find you
spend an inordinate amount of time looking closely
upon feathers and beaks, the perch and flight
of the most common sparrow. Why do you devote
hours building small tables to hang in trees, acorns
mulled over to delight a woodpecker as much as yourself.
Take up the wooden sword with Laertes and Rosencrantz
and Guildenstern—I hear them slapping in the courtyard,
voices crowing *Schadenfreude* at missed lunges,
falls on rears. Too close you are to your mother's
nape, she knitting you a warm sweater and mittens to spend
icy time with gulls off the cliffs, your scope trained on
birds' faces as if their countenance provided company
superior to your royal tree growing to count your every year.

Hamlet Hunting

See how you like the slings
and arrows now, Hamlet, go
to the park among the trees
where squirrels play with hard
nuts, see if you can hold steady
and knock one dead, or aim for limp
like indecision, so you can grab it
by bushy tail—unless you do let go,
looking into its big, deep eye,
a sore in your Rorschach-blotted mind,
leaving everyone but you safe,
your uncle in his pelted *inamabilis sciurus*
costume for *Fasching*, lent of your mind
dry as the springs of Ophelia's brook not.

Sexist Pig

Claudius and Gertrude in their damp Danish
castle, house full of guests, with that Whippet
Hound Hamlet sniffing about—if a dog he would
be sure to pee on the rugs out of spite—and then
Ophelia, traipsing about listening to that
pompous Polonius discoursing on virginity
before exchanging "Neither a borrower nor
a lender be" with his male heir—is any relief
in sight, is Gertrude's bedding Claudius an act
of feminist empowerment or subjugation,
I just cannot get out of this weedy garden
and mucky-mud brook—if I wore a soaked
dress or shiny armor I would be screwed
either way, waiting for Fortinbras *interruptus.*

The Platform

Roaming sea and scary cliffs,
likely bad lightning round midnight,
guarding friends only half-holding
onto Hamlet, empty speech of warning
as if caring or caring as if warning,
Hamlet skips to another part of "the platform,"
and we are supposed to marvel at his father's
ghost out for a walk, refreshing dark after
daylight flames, a bitter son of a bitch
urging his son to buck up, take a stand
against the poisoner now in bed with his widow.
And Hamlet, making no promise but exchanging
falconer language with Horatio, taking the easy
way out going to pray, any excuse not to hunt prey.

Sailor

I have sailed in my small boat below
the cliffs of Elsinore, looked up to see the gray
mass of home I call a castle; where
dim-witted and corrupt officials walk the halls
decked with portraits and shields and spears
and holders of torches. Where is my moral-compass-
blind uncle, jumping on my mother like a beast
in her chamber, or head drooping before the fire
place, belly and bladder full of mead, so sure servants
will clean up any mess he makes. Intellect is a stranger
sitting next to him, the fire too hot to endure for long,
as it rises like a ghost, walks past him, and moves,
this spirit through castle walls and down the cliffs
where I sit in my boat and shape unpleasant thoughts.

Hamlet Swims Laps

I dream of ancient Rome, where I might have a clear pool,
a lane to follow up and down, fifty meters, hark! the metric system
rules, and when I watch the tiles through my clear goggles
below and before me, I count them, so that I know four in the center
are black surrounded by four on each side to send me along an arrow
that makes sense while I sort what could be calmed down: My explosions
at my uncle inside my head, my waste of clever spitefulness at Polonius,
my seeking of quick relief with Ophelia for which regrets come after
the spray, and when I propel myself sleek like an otter and turn with splashes,
I marvel in a pool of happiness, to set again my mind ahead on course
to swim another length, dreams of my mother impure as trunks fill with water,
and then my mind switches to swimming in the cold and dark moat
of my Danish castle, choosing the night of liquid instead of rip-tide currents
clear off the coast, ready to carry me off like some salmon spawned out in death.

Hamlet and the Tooth Fairy

No little doorknobs or pivoting handles
for Hamlet losing his baby teeth.
Anchor an iron chain to the big
knocker outside the boy's quarters,
attach a link of cat's gut to the tooth.
Slam the door, Gertrude, vanish your son's
little hickey-maker, and when he bleeds
praise him with salt water to rinse
the mouth, though little good it did,
his tongue darting to and fro for the whole
world to know centuries later, your son's hands
able enough to get him into trouble, writing
orders to delay his execution, die by sword,
fate just as rotten-ratty as curtained Polonius's.

Legacy Scholarships

I woke up thinking of Hamlet saying, "I speak to you today
via the BBC wireless," and it was in the current Queen Elizabeth's
voice, all so controlled, and he went on, "we stand together as Wittenberg
alumni, you in the fires worse than those licking my uncle's every part,
and I wish to tell you how much I relish your account of cuffing
the pope, no trope can make up for your deed, and my studies were,
as you know, cut short by family business and points more lethal
than dueling tongues, not one drop of the poisoned wine necessary
to quench my life." And then the Queen's voice continuing, so
recognizable with imminent urgency and pronouncement already
forecast, "I have decided, dear Faustus, that we endow a scholarship
in our names, and the recipients must not wear tights, not even in formal
presentation ceremonies, as certain as your name comes before mine in the
alphabet, and it will be all for the united study of theology and politics."

Hamlet Gets a Puppy

You half-sat, half-lay in a basket
with hay fresh from the stable
where you had been whelped by
the foot of the King's favorite cow,
Elsie. I reached out a finger, then two,
and you licked as I bowed my head
over your little warm presence, big ears,
snooter wet, to rub your head and nape!
Somewhere I imagined a star falling
and shining, wisdom coming like
a present, only I was too young to grasp
all this, just that you needed to be scarfed
by my princely garments, and we held onto
each other, I having the footman fetch milk.

Hamlet 2.0

Don't ask me such a stupid question
when we fish for trout if hooked they suffer,
just be grateful that you have the good fortune
to have rights to land and none of the troubles
of a farmer plowing a field with rocks before sleep
and you always know how you will die in the end,
no, this version 2.0 of Hamlet, fresh start, is not
that easy and you should know that, if you read
carefully the last word of the first six lines—
I did not have the right stuff to write something
having nothing to do with the famous soliloquy,
so many men have landed on the moon before,
so many still dream all will start up again,
and I say, do if you do, damned if you don't.

Yorick in Bloom

To begin afresh, even as I smell
the moldy earth that held Yorick's
skull, somewhere in the back of my
mind, and in the future/past gapes
the death of Harold Bloom, as if that
would ease anxieties. No, I am Hamlet's
brother, I am Hamlet, and I am someone else.
Today the Blue Jays were shrieking
through the yard, flying with power
and hard beats of wings, one of us watching
them feed off the bread. Hamlet said
Claudius took his father, pronoun reference,
full of bread, getting a puppy calmed me, him/
Hamlet for such a brief time, time not mine to wind.

Hamlet Gets Married

Forget the muddy death of Ophelia,
muck purple prose poetry of Gertrude
sexualizing dead men's fingers on her body.
The gown soaking up water and pulling her
down, it floated up and over Ophelia's head,
forming an air pocket for breath so only
those prudish viewing her exposed lady parts
fared poorly, or so they say. That mermaid-
moment of Ophelia's—it lasted, so Hamlet
and she stood side by side, he never got
to grave-tumble with Laertes but instead to roll
with her, the courtly priest was prevented from
grumbling about burying a suicide, instead fuming
over man marrying mermaid, deflowered before.

Wishes for Hamlet

It would be in poor taste to say, "Splish, splash,
I was takin' a bath," but Gertrude said Ophelia
was singing snatches of old tunes, the fingers
of dead men there, you remember, but no
less appropriate than the grave diggers singing,
jawing away with flesh about skulls that held
tongues, Hamlet intruding like a curious bird,
unwilling to let go of death swooping down on
everyone, Alexander, all sorts of less distinguished
folk, and alas, poor Yorick, the fool of his father
that Hamlet remembers kissing smack on the lips.
If only Hamlet had been a clown, condemned
to the pleasure of digging graves on stage,
his mind filled with splish-splash before exeunt all.

Hamlet Ice-Skating

For every step you scratch into the ice
you think you can push away the anger
over your father's death. You cannot.
Accept the sorrow of revenge, a task
ahead as unpleasant as having no mittens
during this long scraping and scratching
journey over a frozen lake that speaks
only to our sense of beauty or the serene,
in existence long before Frost stopped by
somewhere with snow falling like postcard
medicine for those as easily afflicted as fooled.
When your ankles tire and you begin to trudge
uphill to the castle, think of your wasted talent,
Frost scratching what you could have in the future.

Morph

Extra! Extra! Read all about it!
Hamlet Revealed as Icarus.
Not that the working foot patrol
would flock to the men and boys
hawking the pulp, toss a coin
in their direction, but for some of us
the revelation that Icarus is Hamlet
is comforting in certainty of uncertainty.
Fly low over the waves, my boy,
flap it up and ride to the sun,
burn brightly or drown darkly,
adverbial bonfire of the vanities
of words swimming and sinking, naked
and dressed on stage, Claudius not your father.

Young and Old

When I first met Hamlet he was an old man full of hope,
so different from his young brooding self, woe-is-me
I-must-avenge-the-death-of-my-father, why the hyphen
can I not outsource this or find someone or something
to rid my being of a tiresome to-do-list hanging
in my mind like laundry needing to be taken off
the clothesline to be folded, pinch me with the pins.
Why could Polonius rat removal not be service enough?
The old Hamlet had fire in his left eye, the kind that comes
from knowing of a journey ahead, expecting the nothing
of an uneventful sleep or blinking transformation into a squirrel.
Into the mind of old Hamlet doing his platform caesuras pounced
abstraction, a squirrel is pelt-real, running with the soul of someone
else, smacking and snacking on mandible's nuts from burial ground.

Mandibular Exchanges Continued

I could not let go of the mandible,
that jaw-piercing gaze Hamlet must
have had seeing Yorick and others
emerge from graves dug while alive
living in a graveyard. Burglarious
mandibles getting in words while
the going is good and bad,
before the silence the old Hamlet
did not fear but the young Hamlet
would have knifed his mother for,
father-ghost instructions or not,
just to get the last word in,
even should it be something un-
magnificent, like I am dying on this pile.

Hamlet Is Painting

like Jackson Pollock today, Ophelia wondering
why he distributes black tears with a giant
instrument that should wand honey.
Tomorrow it may be Edward Munch,
Scream the easy way out for both Hamlet
and Ophelia, worshipers of a wrecked boat
with a man surrounded by sharks, never mind
what the critics might say about Winslow's
oil, the two lovers, or are they not, should
be Winnie the Pooh and Tigger, let sweetness
beat murky overdoing, or if that is not a fit,
let Edward Hopper paint Ophelia nude
while Hamlet is the gas station attendant,
vested-up, pump-fingering, o what could have been.

Hamlet and Mickey Mouse

The two did meet, albeit in earlier
likeness for the Disney-dip of a mouse.
Steamboat Willie a little more dignified,
and when he transported the crazy-eyed
young Dane bound for diverticular England
with appendages Rosencrantz and Guildenstern,
this Ur-version conceived by Disney stopped
his silly whistleblowing, no one else out to sea
to demand his animated stunt. What happened
on water has never been verified by anyone—
I repeat, never been verified by anyone—
Hamlet and Steamboat Willie partners and exiles,
no one to watch Hamlet sign and seal the execution
briefs, drama not supervising for a moment in this space,
ship tossing to and fro, green-gilled creations rising
to bend over the railing, no director ordering them to do so.

Christmas, Hamlet at the Mall

At the mall, where nothing is sadder than
the sound of employees in caged stores
running vacuum cleaners in anticipation
or defeat of foot traffic, a safe Christmas
song can be heard in the section with the
track layout, the locomotive and two short
cars to ride, the all aboard given by a senior
citizen who had a choice of teaching one more
year of school or carrying along children this
commerce way. If you look carefully, beyond
the two children riding unwisely this holiday
train, mothers with smartphones capturing
the event as if it were the first moon landing,
Hamlet sits quietly riding, a third car after all.

Hamlet and the Birds

Woodpecker hammering away, young Hamlet's
room facing the forest where he can
see the tree. Each time he sticks his head out
the bird takes a break. One time climbs up
the trunk, hops and flies a meter, up, then down.
Hamlet is tired and does not want to hear
the woodpecker working on a cavity higher
than his abode. So much appears to go into
excavating a hole in oak, the thoughts continue
in prostrate Hamlet's head, he opens eyes
and sees on the wall facing his bed a stuffed
magpie his father trapped for him. Let its
folklorist cunning be a lesson to you, what kind
I do not know, like burning fingers on a hot pot.

Hamlet Remembering

Rush of water in the ears, sun on the warm head,
dream in the afternoon dozing where a king did not,
while you count the many ways brooks treat a person,
fish to eat, pebbles to skip, cold drink to have, balance
and slip or not, lie flat on your back until you have had
enough and realize wetness more as you stand up to
head for shore. So much depends on a brook or not,
excuses or none to W.C. Williams, and Hamlet remembers
lying on the shore with Ophelia, reciting bad poetry
at which she, good natured and less educated, squealed
with delight, he holding her at arm's length or not,
depending on how either one wishes to remember it,
and then the ears' imagination forgets about the rush
of water and the sun is too warm on the head to remember.

Hamlet and Armor

Trying on his father's armor would be too movie going corny,
either that he must fit into it or he is not large enough.
Taking it off its rack is not a useful choice, Hamlet walking
by it, pacing to and fro in his room, each time reaching metal
destination knocking on its breast plate, not knowing if his
knuckle touch is meant to be playful or angry or how does it
come across, should that decision be made by viewers having
access then not to his face but closeup of knuckles and metal
only, or pull wool over the viewers' eyes by showing Hamlet's
face in pain, repeated knockings enough to make anyone happy
or sad, and could we have another option, a scene to convey
perchance if he feels anything, nothing being something,
he hears the horses coming across the drawbridge, sees in his
mind the dirty moat, knows when his father reigned it was clean.

A Touch of Hamlet-Brother

If Shakespeare had a sister, Hamlet had a brother.
This lad had blond, curly hair, Nordic stereotype,
though the curls were unusual. They so delighted
Hamlet's mother, his brother's curls, that Hamlet
was persona non grata. His mother would always
run her ringed fingers through the boy's hair
to show off to the ladies in waiting and anyone
who came to visit. "Are his curls not beautiful,"
Mrs. Hamlet said, and then, as if troubled by
responsibility, added, "Helga, will you feed
the tyke (and everyone knew the tyke was Hamlet)
his porridge, and let him have a squirt of milk
if he has not wet himself." All this, of course,
explains it part why Hamlet turned out the way he did.

The Way It Is Written

Hamlet dipping nib of ink as if drops were sweat on his forehead,
his thoughts run no faster than the feather of goose alternating
glimpse of the contact quill makes with sheepskin, though he
should use cheaper surface on which to write, but the skull
is a poor substitute for something that lies flat, and Rosencrantz
and Guildenstern's hides were not saved to be engraved.
Hamlet thinks about it, he has it all wrong, his uncle had to play
second fiddle to his brother, Hamlet and his uncle have a connection,
sympatico, why not whack a brother if the shade is too much
in rainy Scandinavia, somewhere in a parallel universe is a play
with Hamlet and his uncle joining forces, locking up brother and
brother, and you can freeze time any way you want, it does not mean one way
will make the food more nutritious, and "Hamlet and His Uncle" is performed
in the future under hot lights in a small theater, look for it, on the Streets of Laredo.

Mulling

I have seen Hamlet pelt with pebbles
squirrels feeding off his tables hanging
in trees to please feathered ones and himself,
the way Hamlet's aim is good to smack
the juicy thigh of the little pelted eaters,
as if Hamlet had gone perverse on the meaning
of slings and arrows he spoke of earlier,
this man-boy or boy-man who could have held
at bay his troubles by filling up the bird baths,
kept puzzles to bird species identification,
stuck to complaints about pale cast when skies
clouded sightings, as if the camera of his eyes refused
to realize a clear picture always must be distrusted,
disdain of such as true as Claudius too easy a target.

Proscenium

Fourteen bars, wrought iron, black,
unshakable, separate him in front
from onlookers. He moves like a caged
tiger pacing back and forth. Every step
and turn, another line and line break
speak aloud in his mind. He hears
every word while also aware of some
of his movement. It is as if he saw
the nib on paper, thumb and forefinger,
the black part of the pen close, move.
The spectators will be silent or vocal,
eat dinner, have drinks. Years ago some
smoked. He is opening act and headliner.
In the wings the dandiness of Siegfried and Roy sings.

Requiem Breakfast

How do I bury Hamlet, perhaps in green eggs and ham,
but I think that not possible because every morning I
see him in my strawberry jam, and I like my strawberry
jam on toast so much, and if Hamlet is not to be held down
by green eggs and ham, and if someone takes away my
strawberry jam, I see Hamlet in my raisin bran, two large
groupings for his eyes, and I stick my finger in the bowl
and make a raisin mouth, gather a few for his nose, because I
do like my Hamlet so much, just like my strawberry jam
and raisin bran, and green eggs and ham, if someone serves
me green eggs and ham, I will know Hamlet is buried in
those words, so why should he not live on in strawberry jam,
in raisin bran, or other breakfast food, no Hamlet will live on,
lucky if he is in green eggs and ham, cease and desist be damned.

Hamlet in Exile

1. Hamlet in Exile

Hibiscus smash. Hamlet on the rocks. On the brink
of self-destruction with drink recipes. We kept it simple
that summer, Hamlet and I, vodka and at first a couple
of crates of tonic water they dropped off for our survivor
exile. I came up with Hamlet on the Rocks, he with my
Hibiscus Smash. Off the wagon, me telling him the term
had to do with conscripts, in what was to be America.
Our hut was covered with banana leaves and it leaked
when the rains washed. Could watch a few large drops
like tarantulas not crawling, but then we were smashed
so the island view became a kind of beach like a garden
we looked upon, raking out memories until we decided
who could eliminate what or whom, not a drop of blood
spilled, the tarantulas of our past fuzzy memories, beginnings.

2. That Play-Thing

I asked him if he did not think that play-thing was heavy-handed.
He told me sometimes you must do things that the masses
will perceive to be their own cleverness, like mentioning a clock
over and over or point to a hand of flesh to foreshadow foregone
conclusions. Like teaching introductory classes now, as opposed
to thirty years ago. Repeat things to the point of being annoyed
by a shrieking parrot not unlike and unlike the one during Edna's
summer vacations on Grand Isle. Speaking of hands, were the so-
liloquies not annoying to deliver, to have to repeat over and over
how indecisive one is, how wronged one has been, and how
the carpe diem of death will have its moment in the future?
I had no choice, he told me. It was either letting words out
on the stage as if it were a river of no return, or muck out stalls,
looking very un-Herculean doing so, shoveling without alliteration.

3. Fever on the Island

I had hoped freedom would come for Hamlet and me,
first on the island, then wherever we went, if we ever
managed to get off that whale's back with the banana
leaves and sand, vodka to last for a lifetime, as if we were
in the land of milk and honey much distorted. Instead,
I had feverish dreams of Ophelia who was suddenly sexy,
and I kept on being visited by my uncle's breath smelling
of boar hunt and old sex, before I cried, then spending
waking and sleeping, who knows which is the waking,
observing my mother and Claudius in coitus, her eyes large
and unexpressive as a fish's, while he kept grunting and wheezing.
The mornings arrived, usually Hamlet was up before me, stoking
the tiny fire that had a pot of bubbling coffee as if in a western movie,
and time kept shifting, just when I thought I had smacked the fly buzzing.

4. Brook

Hamlet was in no hurry to leave the island.
He said he had found a good brook, which meant
it had birds drinking from it so he could watch them
from behind a tree or sitting still with his feet
in the water. Only one day hope showed itself to me
when Hamlet returned from the brook in fine antic form.
The parrots had been fighting and when one bit the other
Hamlet thought its feathers were Ophelia's gown, the brook
was suddenly *the* brook, the tarantulas from our memory
raking on the beach were crawling through his circuits
like electricity. H2 (that's what he called me), I want us
to get off this island immediately, he let out with a shriek
as if he had been transformed into a Blue Jay. Now now,
I said, nap like your father and I will watch over you.

5. Hamlet Ignites

Today it was you who had slept awake in the night, words
in confusion making sense: The only way off the island
is by killing him. You ran without waiting for me to follow
inland, gathering wood and some rocks, repeated trips,
making sense for me with incredible stamina and the command
to gather driftwood for the funeral pyre. The effigy was the Bard.
Kill the Bard! you cried. Tears, as if you were setting your own
house on fire, everything you stood for must come tumbling down.
Your metaphorical suicide, sputtering of Graves's "The thundering
text, the sniveling commentary," was my handkerchief, getting ready
to be roasted and toasted by some critics. A twig from the measly
kitchen fire at the banana leaf hut was all it took: Rome burning, a bush
aflame, the way I imagined Robert Lowell manic, as you fell to the ground,
yammering like a testy child, "I burnt my fingers, I burnt my fingers!"

6. The Ride

I wish I could say the helicopters came, heroic with Wagner music included, *Apocalypse Now* movie a la mode for us, but it was one rescue chopper making economic sound of blades and the medic was all business, methodical, and soon we were up in the air, not even a view of the island I knew we would never see again, you lying on the cot, sedated and held by belt, while I wondered what will he do, I do, upon return to civilization. Best of medical healthcare for Hamlet, a teaching gig for me to finish enough years to have a portfolio to live comfortably in this age of increased life expectancy. How I could not be thinking I will write about Hamlet and me in some capacity, even a poetry book Americans do not flock to, and as I looked out the chopper window, I saw angels, so many of them: Roethke, Bishop, Heaney, Jarrell, Simic—room here permits me to name them all, but I will not—and as we approached the hospital on a larger island, despite good intentions, I invoked: *To be, or not to be: that is the question: Whether 'tis nobler in the mind to suffer the slings* [helicopter lands here].

Hamlet and Laertes

We stood opposite each other, like figures
on a chessboard, only eye-to-eye, as if two
pawns were at the same level holding off
the king, waiting to be slaughtered, no different
from pigs, only purple crow-blood was to be spared.
We had come down to this level, Laertes and I,
bishop or rook or knight more suitable pieces
under conventional circumstances. But this was
anything but, even zig-zagging lines of hesitations
or travels through Europe somehow linear—
all to attend burials and vestiges like duels—
the game stacked like a deck of cards for commoners,
the rush in our heads when the poison kicked in the only
elevation of what had been a low blow from the Bard.

Hamlet and Dickey

Surely there was a heaven for animals—James Dickey
for one would say so in poetic manner one day—
and the way everything was done in slow motion,
even if the outcome was predictable, it was all so
beautiful and comforting to watch the standing up
again when death had befallen these creatures God
calls animals. Had I only been given the chance
to be an animal—had we all benefitted from Dickey's
gift—my father would still be alive, my uncle could have
poured poison in his ear and had other satisfaction with
my mother, Polonius might have gotten the rat's prick again,
Ophelia could have had a cold bath of attention over and over,
the diggers should have unearthed Yorick's skull in looped play—
but Rosencrantz and Guildenstern—may they rot irretrievably.

Hamlet to Horatio

Horatio, Horatio! I have not written about you
because you matter to me the most, it is as if
mentioning you would be unfair in a way
a poet should not write about his children,
for fear that something is misunderstood
or causes a lifetime of unrepairable rift.
So let me take this opportunity to play it
safe and tell you only, thank you, thank you,
for standing by me all those years and until
the end, state my gratitude for what could
have been if I had followed your code—
but you knew by instinct from birth I was doomed,
might have saved us all some time if I had jumped
the platform, a bad joke for you as thanks, my friend.

Hamlet and the Church

I did not know what to make of the clean,
white-washed stone church, its pews hard,
cross simple, only a baptismal, also made
of stone, at the altar. Here I was christened,
even my memory likely not affected by
the touch of priest and parents' hands,
water no halo around my bare head,
the angelic completely absent in my life,
the road of the rational and imagination
mixing in what to outsiders looked like
battle. I would have had it no other way,
only wonder if I should have made plans
to return to the small church yard by the coast
with gravel crunched by the feet of the living.

Bernardo, Francisco, and Marcellus

What ever happened to Bernardo, Francisco, and Marcellus?
A law firm. Where have all the flowers gone. Pete Seeger's
album has a collage of a dove. For all we know the three
could have gone into battle and lost their lives, political
cannon fodder back when they used cannons, or they might
have been promoted to supervisors of the night guards.
I hear one ran an inn for years with a special ale named
Don Quixote, lamenting Picasso saw it fit to draw that fool,
instead of Hamlet. Francisco, as his name promised, really
did enter the church. Marcellus took people on tours
in the Amazon, until he got killed by a poisoned dart
from an excellent blowgun. One thing the three had
in common was that the greatest event in their life
appeared to be the ghost of Hamlet's father, *ubi sunt*.

Horatio's Cock

Such hogwash—*the cock is the trumpet*
to *the morn*. I have this second-hand,
mind you, but I must think you spoke
before an audience not yourself, Horatio.
You and I could have made up better
sayings with animals and the world,
you my editor of flights of fancy.
The Woodpecker of Sorrow. Blue Jay
of Greed. Sparrow of Hideout. Owl of
See-Me-Not. Remember the Vulture
of Clean Living. I always wanted to
rewrite the speeches, but such is not
the luxury of even a well-dressed puppet.
Familiarity on strings breeds tangled contempt.

Hamlet on Writing

I dream of a new Hamlet,
myself in the third person.
With vowels and consonants
tooting and clicking, but
at a lower level where the toot
is not overly loud, the clicks
a pleasant inducement to rhythm.
Castle carp in the moody moat
a bit much, and the aahs and oohs
should be kept to a bearable decibel
reading. I do not want to hear Polonius
friction-toeing around on carpet, nor are
the aahs of Coitus Claudius and Gaudy Gertrude good
for the volume. Give me something drivable, Muse.

Blueberries with Yorick and the Boys

Picking blueberries with Rose and Guild.
Beloved Yorick took us boys, each
carrier of his own basket and what looked
like a comb with much room between
its teeth. I had thought it would be hand
to mouth activity. Not so. Draw the comb
through the leaves of the plant and harvest
a feast of berries all at once: It was cheating,
like flying a kite put together by the
prisoners in the damp dungeon of our castle.
They never saw daylight again, while I
harvested pure air, pure air, the tailed
beast sailing my dreams, every pull
of more line a reminder of confinement.

Spray of Surf

My father taught me to hunt. Allusions
from the Greek myths, poetry by
the Germans, how to fashion a bobber
for fishing on the spot. I was raised
to befriend allusions, in time becoming
an allusion more than others around me.
I tried to become real and dull—
I had plenty of role models to try on—
but I decided to spend much time
sailing my boat off the coast of
Elsinore, wind in my hair and face,
spray of surf the occasional confirmation
I was real, like a dayfly, before I plunged
into allusions head first, dangerous in dreams.

Hamlet and His Tutor

How I hated my tutor, his pedantic
penchant, passion for plus-plus-plus perfect,
the chime of the study clock requiring
all other clocks in vicinity to chime
synchronically. Spelling and organization were
more important than content. Once, I wrote
on the topic of war and I orchestrated
a mouse and rat in combat, arguing the rat
was beastly, the mouse sneaky.
"No no no!" he screamed, slapping my royal nape,
"this essay is about war. You must tell of the armor,
the horses, the phalanx of Romans, the pride
of the warrior that deserves a statue."
His marks penetrated like lashes the ink of my words.

Charles Simic Hamlet (Guilty Pleasure #1)

A draft from a cold room
has Hamlet visit me in a sleep.
He is a curious bird, like a spoon
that is the monster of my childhood.

Outside the wind blows and calls
the name of Hamlet, while we
huddle in the cold of my squeaky bed.

Billy Collins Hamlet (Guilty Pleasure #2)

The snow fell ever so softly
outside my window, NPR
on the BOSE Surround,
a sad and happy jazz tune.

When I walk around
the house I am thinking
of Hamlet, *The Apple
That Astonished Paris*

so many years ago.
The years have feet,
and now my hands
cannot play it again,
like Sam's ditty in *Casablanca*.

William Carlos Williams Hamlet (Guilty Pleasure #3)

Man in tights
you cannot resist

a fire engine or plums
and if I had to do it over

again I would not embark
on long speeches

but keep close to women
in state of half undress

and leave the chickens
outside

while Fragonard
brushes a Hamlet painting.

Elizabeth Bishop Hamlet (Guilty Pleasure #4)

He takes a long time,
our Hamlet, a ride
in five acts with seats
too formal to snore,
and gossip has no room
during this performance
as we are journeying
toward our final
destination. A strange
animal this work,
long as a fish but
maybe not the right
shape. We watch
impatiently waiting
for the end, but want
to show also some
respect to this highly
decorated literary event.
Suddenly I hear a woman
unwrap a cough drop,
and I decide I must
be patient with Hamlet,
so I am good, so I am good.

Two Fellas

Cheek to cheek—his left—
they touch, much too clean
is his, Yorick's skull positioned
just so—narcissism of the actor
and a photographer egging him on.
Yorick still has a decent set of
teeth, ones in the middle missing
as if to spit tobacco. Such large,
round cavities for eyes. And the
hole where the nose used to be
is larger than I expected. I pray
Yorick's nose was not enlarged from
sniffing so much of the rotten,
let the vain actor do more than touch play dirt.

Marvelous (The Rat Stays in the Picture)

How marvelous "I'll lug his guts
into the other room." Such joy to
a measured play, a farewell of beauty
to sty-bed Mother. Hitchcock would
have had a belly laugh and burp
at that one. I can see him directing
Hamlet to get close to the face
of his mother, like that kiss in the *Manchurian
Candidate* between Angela Lansbury and Tony Perkins.
A feat of anger to disguise lust,
entrails clues all over the castle,
Claudius and Gertrude too dim witted
to find Polonius. Fetch the dead rat—
he must lie in honor in the chapel to complete the picture.

In the Woods

Here they slither on green, Danish grass.
The wood is ripe with chanterelles, families
mushrooming amidst bloom of marsh flowers,
Hamlet out mixing with the locals, a regular
ancestor to Prince Harry. Children ask parents
if the mushroom before them is safe to eat.
One father begins to explain, and the mother slaps
hands off in answer. Hamlet chats with
an elder, "When I was a child, the woods were
filled with mushrooms, something is happening."
Pools of light on stumps and stones, sun the gift
for addled fangs. A rosy-cheeked, big boy
has cut a stick and now is the snake-beater.
Had he only and only thrashed R and G in the sun.

Ghost Back

Had my father died of natural cause
I think he would have enjoyed being
a ghost in our castle. Had I had children
I think he would have played with them,
letting them ride on his ghost back,
pretending to buck as my pretend child
laughed in acting. But my father was killed
by poison like chemo and cancer in one,
and now his ghost is dead, visiting my mother
maybe on some nights, but I think I did not think
it was her I saw scrubbing the marker in the rain,
tears washed away in harsh weather—it must have been
my grandmother's ghost taking what she thought was her
rightful place, chained forever, keeping it all in the family.

Life With Hamlet

For weeks you tortured me. Waited on my
doorstep as I came and went to two classes
in the afternoon. Mornings and early evenings
you lay in a thin text carefully extracted
and stapled from the anthology on the kitchen
table so I would not forget to pack you and still
keep the physical weight of my bag light.

You were flesh and blood, and paper and ink.
My notes in red so I could see better passages
I wanted to discuss with my students, blue
fountain pen ink deadly to anthology pages.
I was holding more and more a soliloquy,
students wondering why I was jumping up
and down over words, words, words

to appear on a test and no more. They dreamed
perchance of Starbucks, smoking pot, having sex,
anything but to be tortured in their daydream
by Hamlet and the professor who had become
obsessed by a literary monster. All literature
was a monster. Grendel in the same course
a little more entertaining, the killing more direct.

American Lit, British Lit, World Lit Surveys in One Semester

At least Roethke could be understood
once the term "ambiguity" had been explained,
the footsteps traced to the meaning of
beating time and being dizzy.

It was all a fuzzy, yet momentary binary
insight, to see the cruel father or the overworked
man who simply drank a little too much
and had large hands from manual labor.

Hamlet and Polonius were not such opposites
after all, prissiness in language and action
a common denominator divided up to get one stuck
in pre-Algebra, travel on a muddy country road way kinder.

Exchanging the Hamlet Birds

Once I put the text away I felt so much better.
My rescue inhaler remained in pockets,
even at home with the confidence I would not
need albuterol, having escaped the Hamlet chlorine.

I was driving with my windows down listening
to songbirds, the ominous shrieks and cries
of hawks left in leaves 655 through 751 of Norton,
and shadows of dark and light turned into color.

Northern Parula, Orange-crowned Warbler,
Pine Warbler, even the Black-and-White Warbler
shone in a kind of technicolor. At night my wife
and I walked the dachshunds, not worried about predators.

How Long Free From Hamlet?

I thought I needed to go back into the thicket
of the text again. Do penance, go on a pilgrimage,
find the equivalent of prickly thorns, mosquitoes,
water moccasins, a swamp that would leave me

at best bootless after entry. Some words blew
in my mind like a wind promising nothing.
The exposed roots of Cypress Trees in the swamp
called my name. The Limpkin, Yellow-crowned Night

Heron, Black-crowned Night Heron, amidst the White
Ibises I was, camera obscura turned right side up
as I listened to the shutter and wondered if the birds
thought that was how I spoke, Hamlet-unbound.

On Killing Hamlet

Just how does one kill, say, Hamlet?
Go the Emily druggist arsenic route,
for rats and allegedly Homer, or engage

in more fancy, high-falutin' Hemlock
of philosophy maneuver, or will a strangle
in a dark alley, a knifing while the headlights

shine, suffice? The problem is
the number of ways being considered,
verb form as passive as Hamlet.

Will one day Hamlet be gone in the journey
of Alzheimer's? Or will those surrounding
and avoiding me not know he still inhabits my head.

The Scene

The glare of light—as if Hamlet
had decided to be part of a Christmas pageant.

He was the man-child, somehow scrunched up
to fit into the manger. As for the wise men,

a triple-vision of Polonius put things
into occluded perspective. The Christ Child

was ex-Machina, a gosling eerily following
in tow, suspended across a lake of mouths agape.

Early Start

The sadness of Hamlet like wallpaper
patterns making their mark on a boy

staying with his grandmother for weeks
during the summer. What should have been

building playhouses out of hay, drinking
thick juice from berries clustering

in her garden, watching the cows grazing,
hearing the cuckoo in the trees surrounding

her house—all this through some reverse
magnifying glass, mirror to the mind of a bookish boy.

Poison

Once, I spoke to the birds as if that was
what St. Francis really had done
with a kind of pre- Dr. Doolittle success.

I wanted to lighten my burden of too much
knowledge, learning like an ingrown toenail.
I turned skyward but found some of the birds

to be too lofty, arrogant, or possessing qualities
I was trying to escape. The long-legged water birds
pointed me in the right direction, some bills sharp,

others sifting through water to find nourishment.
They saved me from a long journey across the sea:
The poisoner had been beneath my nose all along.

Hamlet Visits the Gulf Coast

The Bard took liberties with my life—
no, he chronicled its demise—
getting only some birds right,
such as the hawk and handsaw,
but about the omission of seagulls
he was o so wrong.

To think I did not commune
with their sharp-beaked faces
and eyes even more accusatory
off the steep cliffs of Elsinore.
But there is no killing-off young
Hamlet, forever

popular with Americans who
do not understand me and heap
praise with footnotes for school
children to have all joy of poetry
taken from them. So let me
set the record straight during my visit.

The Ring-billed Gulls in my time
I did not know would scavenge
the Gulf Coast, sharp eyes unable
to distinguish plastic and glass
from spring-breakers caring not
if insides tangle to death after
their petite mort on sand and rocks.

Hamlet Reads the Comics

I have taken to reading comics.
There is a guy named Peter Parker
and his Uncle Ben is murdered.
Sympathy, empathy, what have you,

and that magical moment of the spider
bite followed by powers to fight crime.
I can relate somewhat—after all, my parents
were killed, though I mourn only my father—

but I really don't like that Spider-Man boy.
People reading his adventures voluntarily,
flocking to movies, buying action figures,
beach towels, I mean, I got the short shrift.

Hamlet Discovers Liquid Soap

Is this the fragrant kiss my father's ear
tasted while he napped kilometers from Eden?
Were it my uncle used this substance more,
my mother less, to shake the kingly bed.
And while we are at it, I could have used
a few bottles to mix with the sea
and applied a coat on deck that Rosencrantz
and Guildenstern slide into gaping waves
like a whale with no way out for Jonah.
Forgive me, I cannot resist, but a few bottles
I must have dispatched to Lady Macbeth,
now would she prefer rose or lemon,
can moisturizer be added for frequent washing.

Hamlet Plays the Guitar

I have always wanted to say *strum*
and strum on through the night
while I hear the owl in the trees
sing along as I strum. *Strum.*
Hoot-hoot. Hoot-hoot. No written
rendition does the sound of an owl justice.
But *strum, strum* sounds so good,
and as I twist the tuning keys, tighten them,
I get a kind of feeling like a pain that is good.
Pressing the fretboard cuts into my fingers
as I strum, strum. The word is so hypnotizing
and deceiving, like calm before a storm.
And out of the sound hole comes something,
but I think about what it would be like to disappear
into it, what secrets it has carried over centuries.

Hamlet on Jeopardy

To click or not to click
to give the answer
is of prominent concern
in this studio of mostly
older viewers. They know
all too well how your life
can change in an instant,
whether they have understood
or misunderstood Frost's
much worn poem.

Hamlet winces at Alex Trebek's
polite-assertive "Pick a category."
The choice offers "Words without
Vowels" and "Dead Ends,"
so even Hamlet lets out a chuckle.
He knows words without vowels,
has pondered them, stringing "h's"
together, h h h h h h, in imitation
of what he fears dying unable to
breathe feels like, on his visit to America.

In Our Hands

These are the hands of Hamlet:
Arthritic, calloused finger where
the quill moved during moonless
nights when he wrote in his diary
the truths of life, not experienced
during full-moon nights but in
brooding contemplation when
the thickness would lift just so
to enable him to write the history
we never saw, the doppelgänger
having fallen before our stage-struck
eyes and centuries of reading
the same play attributed to Shakespeare.

Before the Burning

It all came to me on a walk in the woods,
after I had turned the 2.5 mile mark
to make for a good fiver. Did the life
of Hamlet really matter when we saw it?
The plot folded like church programs
before the collection plate like a prediction.
No, the Hamlet to know was the one alive
before his father's alleged putting to sleep
like some royal dog poisoned by the cur
of Hamlet's uncle. I saw Hamlet the years
before and I said a little yippee out there
on the trail in the woods where only birds,
hogs, snakes, and what I could not see
were my companions, before the burning.

Eggs

I did not know any better,
thinking collecting birds' eggs
was no theft, unburdened
by knowing the birds yet:
My father taking me to the stable
where we climbed a ladder and got
swallows' eggs. I collected them,
what remained after blowing out
the wet center, a darkness I never
saw, because the inside of the egg
did not show anything where a small
hole was pricked. My shelves were ripe
with aviators' offspring that could have been.

Falconry with Father

Falconry with father I call it out,
looking back with alliterative tilt,
you and me and the birds on horseback.
It was never about killing prey for me.
I loved the flight, spread of the wings,
and the marvelous maneuvers no human
can ever hope to experience, Icarus be
proof and damned. I did not like the falcons
were hooded, Crown of Denmark no burden
that should be embroidered upon a bird's
blinding cap. Thank God you skipped the gawdy
amber my uncle sported on his birds' heads.
The look immediately after the hood was lifted
pained me and the re-placing at the end of the hunt
was omen of swirling wants and denials, fodder for my journal.

Hamlet's Bard No. 2

I do not pretend to be Thomas Wolfe
nor was meant to be the man
with the fruit crates said to dump
stacks of papers with inspiration
and labor to have the poor editor
best old Hercules.

What started as immersion
in Bard No. 1's text, in the employ
of a place called university
where I taught three sections of the play
in the season called semester,
turned into co-fettering of 14 lines,

a wish to respond to a man who lived
below the country in which I was born.
No Hamlet for the Swede with the nib
intent on doing penance in a form
of sonnet he had admired but could not
stand for over fifty years.

Now take this gathering like Frost's
promise and exultation to join him
on the pasture, the light of the study
for sure casting a shadow where tired
hands type up the manuscript after
apple-picking Hamlet, fresh and bruised.

Fireside Chats with Father

We did not exchange lines
in iambic pentameter.
Nor did we make clever
phrases mixing up
the auditory and visual.

It had nothing to do
with Roosevelt. He was not
a borrower of the phrase
but might have lent it
through time travel

to me. While the flames
cooked our shins,
my father instructed me
about the spine, standing
tall and behind every word

flying out of my mouth.
He also told me he knew
I was sensitive and must
work on incorporating that
in life but not bury it.

Visiting Polonius's Greenhouse

Life was not always bad with Polonius.
I remember when I was seven
and he took me into his greenhouse,
told me all about a Roman emperor

who had to eat cucumbers to stay well,
and they built a *specularium* to grow
the unseasonable year round.
I beheld the blooming of a flower

while outside my face had been numb
from walking, and the winds threw
caution to hell, as I followed our court's
advisor. Nothing politic back then,

but late at night when I rock in my chair,
lower back aching, thoughts pulse
about the irony of it all, talker Polonius
erecting a greenhouse, caster extraordinaire.

Travels with Father

The aqueducts the Romans built inspired awe
in my father, who held forth about the ingenuity
on display from so many centuries ago.

Everything came alive when he told me
on our visit to the continent about the circuses,
bread and games, arenas filled with water,

ships doing battle, gladiators brutally fighting.
My father was an educated man, smart, King
of Denmark, for God's sake, but the barbarian

in him relished antiquity, like a promise of
what might still come, even for descendants
of the Vikings, all now throttled.

Hamlet as a Roofer

Poor fellow, just not cut out
for the job. Marcellus and Bernardo,
they can cover much ground
on the roof under a scorching sky,
especially if Horatio serves as foreman.
Hamlet and the nail gun, that hesitancy,
a delay and disaster waiting to happen,
approaching the roof's edge. Hamlet,
must you speak to that gray squirrel
with hypnotizing gaze? Know his soul
will lead you astray, climb down,
have a coffee and Danish, *wienerbrød*,
and for God's sake do not attempt,
¡Ser, o no ser, es la cuestión!

Hamlet in Texas

It does not look at all like Denmark,
though the Panhandle in winter
will do with its snow. Hamlet is traveling
by pickup truck, a Danish Country Reporter
lost among the many grand things this state
has to offer. If they could see me now, Hamlet
thinks, a little jig as if fencing Laertes while
trying on a cowboy hat in the store that has
a mirror for hats and another one for boots.
He settles on a fine pair made with Rattler skin,
though they remind him of his father across the sea
having poison poured in his ear by Uncle Claudius.
Next stop is the gun shop built like a fortress.
A six-shooter will do to ward off any harm, real or imagined.

Hamlet and the Critics

I never liked the way they liked me:
Intellectual, Freudian mama's boy,
preserver of Ophelia's virginity.

I was a bad boy, trapped in tights
and pentameters, monologues
audiences counted when I was put out

to text. Who did they think they were,
the scholars condemning me for hesitations,
themselves having it one way one day,

another next month when a colleague
published something about my "life."
Petty cowards, buying into the play

as if it were life or a mirror to it.
Why, if you held one to their mouth
their air would fog it quicker than common sense.

Netflix Hamlet

Grand sets—cold stone castle
with visuals to heat to temperature
of tropics.

Lots of fucking—Claudius and Gertrude
naturally, but also small people,
and Hamlet

and Ophelia engaged in chaste acts,
maybe rolling around in flowers
and garlands.

The voyage across the sea
will be talked about by viewers—
no expense spared

since a second set has to be built,
might as well make it
worth the dollars and euros.

Rough sailors and a look on Hamlet's
face as if they make him more
than sea sick.

Rosencrantz and Guildenstern
fettered in irons with the brutality
of whacked heads.

The *Crown of Denmark* bleeds for
attention with *Fleabag, Game of Thrones,*
viewers suckers.

A Poem for My Uncle

When I was young I was very angry,
publicly, about my mother shacking up
with my uncle. I just could not get over it.
Little did I know, things were not as well
in that Garden as I thought. I am not talking
about the poisoning, filling up my father's
ear so he would die in a vile and clever way.
I think Mom and Dad were just staying together
for the sake of me, until I would be all grown up,
and that was taking too long, you know that.
Yes, even back then parents did stupid things
for their children, and most kids are smarter
in the practical compartment than I am.
They know when parents should part ways.

With Cherry on Top

It dawned on me, as the saying goes,
and who says you can't use certain
sayings in poetry—why clichés cannot
be the boon that is like the cherry on top
of the ice cream Sundae as if anyone
I know these days eats one or has tasted
one in years. What dawned on me,
to get back on track, is that I would take
my revenge not with poisoned tips or
lips spouting clever things about rodent
Polonius. Ah-ah! Say things in a very
deliberate way, stop the music expected
from so much poetry. Slow down
and tell it like it is, yes, that is a reference
to a song, and as I hit *Wikipedia*, I learn something:
"Chinese talk show aired from 1996 to 2009."

Reporting Live

This is Hamlet self-reporting from the Castle.
I have just come down from my mother's smelly
chambers, and the people I talked to here intimate
that she indeed has a nightly visitor. Senior officials,
while not commenting publicly, seem to indicate
that this is indeed the Uncle of Hamlet, myself. I am trying
to get a live shot here of the scene—Sam if you would
pan—thank you, and you can see, Anderson, the castle
is both a lively and dead place. There is a kind of stench
in the air, something ominous, and Anderson, now back
to you, this is Hamlet reporting live from the Castle, CNN.

Lost Laredo Poem

I can't find the poem anymore. I left it in some unmarked
file, document 28 or what have you—you can relate I am sure—
but it was good in that I had "Hamlet" being performed on
the streets of Laredo, and I don't think it had this addition
that occurred to me just now: Piñatas were hanging off
an old coat rack—as if anyone uses one anymore—and
the audience of liquor-fortified tourists got to get up
and whack the shit out of the papier-mâché creations
made in the image of characters out of "Hamlet."
The audience that was left seated with nothing to destroy
had a real vicarious thrill once each piñata would open.
Beer poured, sometimes wine, and from one tequila.
I have never seen so many mouths at the teat one way or another.

Ophelia Reads the Confessional Poets

I am not Jarrell in drag,
though I have been seen
in the market in town.
I do pluck flowers,
but they are not chosen
to express emotions
that brand names have stolen.
I do not mourn for kisses
gone or lost in the future
from Hamlet. I do not want
a young lad of lower class
to lust after me. I am not worried
about my funeral coming up soon.
I am, after all, still a young woman
and not Randall Jarrell in psychic drag.

Phonebook Troubles

If you were to look for me in the phone book,
as if a decent phone book existed anymore,
you would find me under "Hamlet," that's in
the H's, and my name would come after
a Mr. Hamle and before a Mrs. Hamllet.
I point this out to you because I have had
over the years challenges with the phone
company and their printing. For years
they got the alphabetizing of names right,
but the passage of time brings the aches
of abuse of spelling, whether intentional
or negligent. So look for me in the H-section,
just plain Hamlet, one name, lie Cher or Beyoncé.
I promise to disappoint much more than the Bee.

Hamlet Watches a Classic Movie (Harry Hamlet)

Celebrating my first Fourth of July in America,
I got to watch *Dirty Harry* on something called
a DVD player.

I enjoyed the movie very much, especially
the rapid transportation in four-wheeled carts
without horses.

But the quotes left me speechless, filled with
envy, how I had missed out. "Go ahead,
make my day."

And: "You've got to ask yourself one question,
'do I feel lucky.' Well do you, punk?" There
was a Hamlet for all seasons!

he still inhabits my head

Do Not Let Go

I never took a liking to you. Your scheme,
and your cleverness showed itself like cleavage
without a face. Your indented, at least in some
appearances, last two lines coupling up like
courtship on display, dispassionate kissing
of "Time's scythe" and insistence on outliving time.
Now Donne and the Petrarchan rhyme scheme
I took to immediately, memorizing the way to go
by heart, and the *volta* was a charge I soon felt coming on
instinctively as I neared the eighth line. I set myself a challenge,
fallen already as if in Marvell's "Coronet," only
not as beautiful, working to build a crown of twigs
to celebrate your Hamlet, as if you had monopoly
and I was collecting play money with dice,
moving around trying to amass something that did not
agree with my temperament or match the Hamlet I prized.

Wish

How beautiful your "Child," meditation of objects
making their gradual appearance without the rapid
fire of Panzer Dad and suicide performance act
pieces. I mean you no harm when I say I prefer
the "Child," the ducks and April snowdrop,
I am sure you did, too. Had there been time,
not the Eliot one drilled into our heads going
Prufrocking, but some more calm talks between
Hamlet and "Hamlet," Shakespeare and Hamlet and "Hamlet,"
a partnership without scratching to fill the pages
and then the theatre, a small performance in the round,
as if waiting for Godot, but with warmth and lanterns,
the kinds that are used to prevent ships from marvelously
breaking instead of showing where the rocks rise and
the destruction will come, o what a Hamlet and "Hamlet,"
o everything could have been, forget the exeunt all like a red fire exit.

Cocktails with Lowell

Cocktails with Lowell, he tells me just to get it all in there,
don't worry about family and friends, you will be hurt anyway,
and if you feel that your mother and father need public censure
in the name of art, sacrifice yourself on the public altar of private
poetry. Who reads poetry anyway who matters. I am trying to get
a word in, while he eloquently yammers as if one could do that,
Abramowitz and that verb, Lowell serving in some prison
that does not have a soccer field on my mind like the kennings
of love-cars and was it a skull-hill, if not, it should have been.
I now want to stuff my own turkey, turn it inside out to look
good for aficionados of cooking shows who either cook
really well or cannot boil water to burn their own fingers,
my hands and tongue will rest, for I am Hamlet meant
to do more than swell the progress of a scene or two,
thank you very much Mr. Eliot Prufrock whomever you are.

Naturerama

Eyes of deer in the dark
where they have come out
on the moonlit pasture,
venturing out just a little farther
than they and I are used to.
A 12-point buck and his lady
companions, as euphemistic
and relationship-defining
as my Uncle Claudius's
carrying on in stonewalled
Elsinore, where the floors
were covered by deerskins
while candles lit not softly
as he engaged with his ladies
on moonless nights, no
music of the wind or frogs,
just bellowing Claudius, *Ribbit.*

Traveling with Hamlet

I travel well in this thing they call an airplane,
forget the magic mats my nanny sang to me
about when winds and snow surrounded
the castle and I was too old to be nursed,
even royal privileges be cursed.

Next to me a man wearing what he tells me
is called an Hawaiian shirt is on his fourth
vodka tonic, pretty little bottles they bring
you, in this territory called first class,
and he says, "Damned right I fly first class."

But what he tells me about the plane being
made out of aluminum crowns all achievements.
I am Danish-proud as I have another little bottle:
aluminum was discovered by a fellow Dane,
Hans Christian Ørsted, no, not the fairy tale guy

you ignoramuses, and while we're at it, did you know
the wind moves faster over the airplane wing so the pressure
on top is less than that on the bottom of the wing, and that
means flight, the kind I am enjoying now, let's order another
round for my new friend in Hawaiian shirt first class.

Coffee with Pinocchio

I ran into Pinocchio the other day at Starbucks—
I am really adapting to my new homeland America—
but the European in me must have made me linger
to drink my coffee, no laptop to finger-dance with,
but thoughts and observing everyone else coming
and going, no Michelangelo, but some coat of arms
coffee mugs available for sale.

That is when I spotted him, Mr. Pinocchio—odd habit
I have picked up here in the South, calling people
by their first name with Mr. in front of it—
and we made eye contact, not in any weird way,
and he sat down, asking if this table was taken,
a giveaway he was European, not afraid to get shot
sharing a table, though he carried a laptop, but we must

not stereotype Europeans and deprive them of their electronic
friends. "You are Pinocchio, aren't you," I said, while he
retorted, "What ever gave me away," in lilt sounding like
"I never promised you a rose garden," as he lifted his head
to take the nose out of the coffee he had been stirring.
"I read you were found hanging from a tree in an early version
of your story," I accused him. "Yes, that has been known to happen,"
he retorted again. And he dove in nose first into his coffee again,
while I drank mine with the cutting plastic lid opening, Americano.

Postcard from America

Dear Danes of alliteration,
Today I drove across the bridge,
a beautiful sight—Americans are said
to jump from this bridge to commit suicide—
and my Hertz rental car has unlimited
mileage, a thing they are sure to regret
because I will drive all across America.
I am planning on visiting Arizona next,
the way I am driving, they will be
out of business one day.
Yours, Hamlet, lover of ketchup
and air conditioning and tabs
I can just throw out the window.

Crayons and Taxicabs

Burnt sienna on the seat,
half of one, the other maybe
in the cab, maybe elsewhere,
the traveler taking it along
after a ride who knows where.

But more crayons have tumbled
in this automobile: I find spring green
(a whole one), mahogany (also whole),
and if I were inclined to reach down
raw sienna and sea green, somewhat

worse for the wear, could be mine.
Who was this traveler who left
what children and adults have used
throughout history, though most recently
invented by Alice and Edwin Binny—

school teachers!—as I read up and learn
from taking this old form of transportation—
no Uber or Lyft, but a lift from knowing
Alice came up with the name, and as the .com
site says: "The trade name Crayola was coined

by Mrs. Edwin Binney who joined the French word
'craie,' meaning stick of chalk and 'ola' from the word
'oleaginous,' meaning oily." And so I travel enriched
by daily find, my escape from Elsinore and formal schooling
in Wittenberg, not places to look for me under your boot-soles.

Hamlet in Kindergarten

I first met Hamlet in kindergarten.
He was alone, by himself, solipsism
his sole companion in the sandbox.

He espied me on the green grass
of Outsider Academy for the Little
Rich People, apart from classmates

playing marbles to augment allowances.
"See these planks here," Hamlet said,
unexpectedly colloquial and democratic,

"they are the figments of boundaries."
He did not look at me directly,
staring into the sand as if it were

a reflection of his mindscape.
Smart beyond years, wet behind
the ears, we were companions

waiting to cross fate, knowing
our sports cars purchased by fathers
were the perfect getaway.

Scapulae

"Ox scapula," Hamlet said to me
in the dark, small-lamp lit library
where we were to conjugate Latin

verbs in our off-time. He was researching
shovels, spades he called them, licking
his lips as he did when coming across

a discovery. "Scapula and spatula,
digging, see the etymological connection?!"
He looked at the knuckles of his hands,

then palms, then me. These hands were made
for researching, turning the pages of books, holding
the quill, callus on left side of right pointing finger.

Hamlet Takes Trumpet Lessons

He soon plays "Taps," proud
of his embouchure and not
needing to press any valves.

He loves the C-E-G notes,
the simplicity of opening up
a mournful sound,

worrying only if he will
be able to sustain the last
long note,

or is doomed as if on
the play's stage, now
a cold cellar of banishment

so the rest of the household
will not have to listen
to his damp overtures.

Mourning Is Such an Imperfect Experience

Mourning is such an imperfect experience,
the crying, the shouting, the doubting,
the anger, the wish to wound someone
and fault oneself, and most of all,
the pain is not to my liking.

Was it really my fault I was not
in my father's garden to stop
poison from entering his ear?
If Uncle Cladius had not done
the dastardly deed, surely

my father would have collapsed
from a bad heart or my mother
would have gotten to him slowly
like rot in the gut as if that would
make up for the way he treated her.

To see him up there on the platform
and be set up to pace like an idiot,
feign religion as a reason not to slay
a man praying on his knees,
mourning is such an imperfect experience.

What Writers Are Saying
about *Hamlet in Exile*

Here, Hamlet is in exile from Elsinore, from his own time in the 13th century, Shakespeare's in the 17th. Now in ours, he is bereft of the soaring iambics and lives not in the language of the spheres but in our words, poor mortals that we are. And in this rebirth, we see him as he always was and will be. Like us, he is caught between the thought and the deed. But in these poems, he mutters, grows old and so is all of us. And in him, we will walk upon the shore and find a seashell and holding it to our ear hear the sea.
—Frank Kersnowski, author of *The Early Poetry of Robert Graves: The Goddess Beckons*

Is there something rotten in Denmark? Perhaps we should ask Hamlet or the transplanted Texan Ulf Kirchdorfer. But neither one asked or answered the question. In "Hamlet Discovers Liquid Soap" Kirchdorfer does ask

> Is this the fragrant kiss my father's ear
> tasted while he napped kilometers from Eden?

And in the poem "Poison," he answers with "The poisoner had been beneath my nose all along."
Some of the poems are witty:

> I never took a liking to you. Your scheme,
> and your cleverness showed itself like cleavage
> without a face.

Some of the poems are wise:

> And: "You've got to ask yourself one question,
> 'do I feel lucky.' Well do you, punk?" There
> was a Hamlet for all seasons!

Most are witty and wise:

> Will one day Hamlet be gone in the journey
> of Alzheimer's? Or will those surrounding
> and avoiding me not know he still inhabits my head.

—Robert Flynn, author of *Standing on the Bottom of the World*

Poor Yorick had nothing on the Hamlet who ambles and sometimes tumbles from the Renaissance into the 21st century in this witty and ironic collection by Ulf Kirchdorfer. The young prince goes fishing, skates on ice, paints, plays Jeopardy and the guitar, muses on the troubles of American poets who, he finds, have spun his anxieties into contemporary webs of contemplation. Kirchdorfer's read his Ernest Jones, and his Hamlet is hung on pricks, pokes, holes, smacks, and snatches.

This collection is a marvel of literary imagination.

—Rob McDonald, photographer, *Carolina Writers at Home*

In these remarkably imaginative and provocative poems Hamlet, that expert time-traveler, is shown once more to be a man for all ages. And through him Kirchdorfer gives voice to the divided and conflicted age that is our own.

—Robert Hamblin, author of *Epiphanies, Large and Small: Collected Poems*

The center did not hold—and that's a good thing—for these sonnets brim with humorous allusiveness and good-natured pokes of recognition. Ulf Kirchdorfer, an unsentimental time-tripper, is now the longest branch on Hamlet's family tree. You'll delight in how he has rewritten the Shakespearean past with a new accent.

—Jerry Bradley, author of *Collapsing into Possibility*

www.ingramcontent.com/pod-product-compliance
Lightning Source LLC
Chambersburg PA
CBHW021507090426
42739CB00007B/510